YOUR KNOWLEDGE HAS

Irena Stotz

Team development. How to assemble a successful team

GRIN Verlag

Bibliografische Information der Deutschen Nationalbibliothek:

Die Deutsche Bibliothek verzeichnet diese Publikation in der Deutschen National-
bibliografie; detaillierte bibliografische Daten sind im Internet über http://dnb.d-
nb.de/ abrufbar.

Imprint:

Copyright © 2012 GRIN Verlag GmbH
Druck und Bindung: Books on Demand GmbH, Norderstedt Germany
ISBN: 978-3-656-56457-7

FOM – University of Applied Sciences Dortmund

Team development:
How to assemble a successful team

Study Program

Master of Business Administration (MBA)

Module: Soft Skills and Leadership Qualities

Author: Irena Stotz

2nd Academic Semester 2012

September 30th, 2012

Table of Contents

List of Figures

1 Introduction

Teamwork is the most important factor in achieving success in competition for companies. Teamwork should support companies to operate effectively and flexibly in the market.[1]

For employee's teamwork is also important; in every job advertisement teamwork is required. And the higher an employee rises on the career ladder, the more important teamwork becomes.[2]

Previously, employees often work in departments, these days in many companies the employees work in project or task orientated teams. The task of today's managers is to build a cohesive and successful team out of a group of individuals. This team has to work together for a specific time and afterwards they will have to work developing new projects.[3]

This assignment highlights successful teams and how they can be assembled and work together. This will be demonstrated in the second chapter using Belbin's team role inventory. To begin with, the different team roles will be described and afterwards the differences between unsuccessful and winning teams will be discussed.

After a successful team is assembled, they are paced through the stages of team development. The most famous model of team development is the five stages by Bruce W. Tuckman, which will be analyzed in the third chapter. Later, the phases of team development will be shown. The limits of this model will also be illustrated.

The fourth chapter summarizes the development of this work.

---

[1] Cf. Eickenberg (2006), p. 67.
[2] Cf. Belbin (2008), p. 9.
[3] Cf. Sueddeutsche.de (2012), w.p.; Managementpraxis.ch (2012), w.p.

2 Belbin's Team Role Inventory

In a unique study at Henley Management College in the 1970s, Meredith Belbin asked the question "What makes some teams succeed, and others fail?" In a ten-year period of observational research Belbin used a simulation to find an answer to this question.[4]

A result of the study was that the most successful companies were those which had a mix of different types of people with a wide range of different characteristics. These different characteristics are referred to as the nine "Team Roles".[5]

"Belbin's team role framework is probably one of the most renowned and currently widely used in a great variety of practical team development and management development purposes."[6]

2.1 Team Roles

The first instance that the term 'team' is used is in regard to games. Every player has a position and a specific responsibility in the team. The skills of each player are important but the strength of the team depends more on how well the players combine.[7]

Beyond this template the term team is also used in industry.[8] In this assignment the definition of a team will be as follows:

> "A Team Role was defined as a tendency to behave, contribute and interrelate with others in a particular way."[9]

Belbin's approach is that team members' behavior does not come only from the position they occupy, but also from a constant dialog process between team members, so that every team member has to define his or her specific team role.[10]

In the following text the nine team roles that are shown in Figure 1 will be described.

---

[4]   Cf. Belbin (2008), p. 25; Belbin (2004), p. 1; Belbin (2000), p. 2.
[5]   Cf. Belbin (2008), p. 25; Water/Ahaus/Rozier (2008), p. 500.
[6]   Water/Ahaus/Rozier (2008), p. 499.
[7]   Cf. Belbin (2010), p. 97.
[8]   Cf. Belbin (2010), p. 97.
[9]   Belbin (2008), p. 21; Belbin (1999), p. 32.
[10] Cf. Aritzeta/Ayestaran/Swailes (2005), p. 159.

Action-oriented Roles			
	Shaper	Implementer	Completer/Finisher
People-oriented Roles			
	Co-ordinator	Teamworker	Resource Investigator
Thinking-oriented Roles			
	Plant	Monitor Evaluator	Specialist

Figure 1: Sussessful Clusters of Behavior[11]

Belbin classified the team roles in three categories. The first category is the action-orientated role. It is based on the position of the employee in the organization and the accompanying responsibilities and authorities. These team roles are the Shaper, the Implementer and the Completer Finisher. The second category is the functional role. This is about the level of experience and expertise. Those are the Plant, the Monitor Evaluator and the Specialist. The third category is the people-oriented role. It takes account of how people make decisions, interact with each other, and how they utilize their talents. These roles are the Coordinator, the Teamworker, and the Resource Investigator.[12]

Plant:

The first Team Role that was identified was the Plant. Belbin called the role plant because one such individual was "planted" in each team. The Plant is highly creative

---

[11]   Source: belbin.com (2012 a), p. 1.
[12]   Cf. Water/Ahaus/Rozier (2008), p. 499.

and good at solving problems in unconventional ways. Other attributes of the Plant are imagination and freethinking. His weaknesses are that he sometimes ignores incidentals and, because of his preoccupation, he is not always able to communicate effectively.[13]

Monitor Evaluator:

The next team role referred to as the Monitor Evaluator. He is a levelheaded person, strategically inclined and a discerning thinker. The Monitor Evaluator weighs up various options in a dispassionate manner and judges situations accurately. But he often has little drive and lacks the ability to inspire others. He can also be over critical.[14]

Co-ordinator:

The Co-ordinator is mature and focuses on the team's objectives. He clarifies goals, he promotes decision-making, and he involves others in appropriate, constructive ways. The Co-ordinator delegates work appropriately. His failings are that he can be seen as manipulative and he offloads his own share of the work.[15]

Resource Investigator:

The Resource Investigator is outgoing and enthusiastic, so when there is a risk that the team will become isolated and inwardly-focused, the Resource Investigator carries the team's ideas to the world outside the team. He develops contacts and provides inside knowledge. But he is also over-optimistic; he loses interest once initial enthusiasm has passed.[16]

Implementer:

Implementers are able to plan a practical, workable strategy and perform it as efficiently as possible. They can turn ideas into actions and they organize tasks which need to be

[13] Cf. Belbin (2008), p. 29 f.; belbin.com (2012 b), w.p.; belbin.com (2012 c), w.p.; Water/Ahaus/Rozier (2008), p. 501; Blenkinsop/Maddison (2007), p. 670.
[14] Cf. Belbin (2008), p. 31 f.; belbin.com (2012 b), w.p.; belbin.com (2012 c), w.p.; Water/Ahaus/Rozier (2008), p. 501; Blenkinsop/Maddison (2007), p. 670.
[15] Cf. Belbin (2008), p. 33 f.; belbin.com (2012 b), w.p.; belbin.com (2012 c), w.p.; Water/Ahaus/Rozier (2008), p. 501; Blenkinsop/Maddison (2007), p. 670.
[16] Cf. Belbin (2008), p. 40 f.; belbin.com (2012 b), w.p.; belbin.com (2012 c), w.p.; Water/Ahaus/Rozier (2008), p. 501; Blenkinsop/Maddison (2007), p. 670.

taken care of. Implementers are very inflexible and they do not like changes, so they are slow to respond to new possibilities.[17]

Completer Finisher:

At the end of a task, the Completer Finisher is needed. He refines the work and looks for errors. He subjects the work to the highest standards of quality control. His further qualities are that he is painstaking, conscientious, and anxious to do well. His weaknesses are that he is inclined to be unnecessarily concerned and he is loath to delegate work.[18]

Teamworker:

The Teamworker helps the team to bond, to use its versatility to identify the work required and to complete it for the benefit of the team. So Teamworkers are, on the one hand, cooperative, perceptive and diplomatic. They are able to listen and avert friction. On the over hand, they are indecisive in difficult situations and they tend to avoid confrontation.[19]

Shaper:

Shapers ensure that the team keeps its momentum. They are challenging individuals and they do not lose their focus or momentum. They are dynamic, thrive on pressure and they have the courage to overcome obstacles. But they are also inclined to provocation and offending other people's feelings.[20]

Specialist:

The ninth Team Role is referred to as the Specialist. This role emerges after the initial research has been completed. His in-depth knowledge of a key area is another essential

---

[17] Cf. Belbin (2008), p. 35 f.; belbin.com (2012 b), w.p.; belbin.com (2012 c), w.p.; Water/Ahaus/Rozier (2008), p. 501; Blenkinsop/Maddison (2007), p. 670.
[18] Cf. Belbin (2008), p. 37 ff; belbin.com (2012 b), w.p.; belbin.com (2012 c), w.p.; Water/Ahaus/Rozier (2008), p. 501; Blenkinsop/Maddison (2007), p. 670.
[19] Cf. Belbin (2008), p. 44 f.; belbin.com (2012 b), w.p.; belbin.com (2012 c), w.p.; Water/Ahaus/Rozier (2008), p. 501; Blenkinsop/Maddison (2007), p. 670.
[20] Cf. Belbin (2008), p. 42 f.; belbin.com (2012 b), w.p.; belbin.com (2012 c), w.p.; Water/Ahaus/Rozier (2008), p. 501; Blenkinsop/Maddison (2007), p. 670.

team contribution. The Specialist is single-minded, self-motivating and dedicated. He provides knowledge and skills which are often in rare supply. But often contributes only on a limited front, and can dwell on technicalities.[21]

2.2 Unsuccessful and Winning Teams

Belbin figured out that certain combinations of team roles performed more successfully than others. In this chapter the results of his study will be demonstrated and the unsuccessful and the winning teams will be described.

In his study Belbin found out that the team with the sharpest analytical minds and the highest levels of experience did not perform better than other teams and sometimes performed worse. One reason is that these group members spent a large time in abortive debate and trying to persuade the others to take their point of view. But these people did not seem to convert others or to be converted themselves. A further reason is that there was no coherence in the decisions that the team reached and several pressing and necessary jobs were totally neglected. The advantages gained by the team from their efforts or brilliance were nullified by their lack of coherent teamwork. Belbin called this phenomenon the "Apollo Syndrome".[22]

Besides the Apollo Syndrome there are some characteristic features of unsuccessful teams. Unsuccessful teams tend to finish last and they "do not necessarily suffer from poor morale poor apparent team work."[23] But the poor morale is not the cause; it is the consequence of failure or of diminishing fortunes. The ineffective teams can be classified into two categories. The first category includes those who are products of their culture so that the faults of the team epitomize the faults to which the company as a whole has long been subject. In such cases a change in the team has only marginal ramifications regarding their effectiveness. The other type of ineffective teams, are

---

[21] Cf. Belbin (2008), p. 46 f.; belbin.com (2012 b), w.p.; belbin.com (2012 c), w.p.; Water/Ahaus/Rozier (2008), p. 500; Blenkinsop/Maddison (2007), p. 670; Aritzeta/Ayestaran/Swailes (2005), p. 161.
[22] Cf. Belbin (2004), p. 9 ff.; Costello (2011), p. 26; Water/Ahaus/Rozier (2008), p. 500; Senior (1997), p. 245 ff.
[23] Belbin (2004), p. 75.

those, which contain unfortunately combined characters. In this case, a change of team members can be a remedy, which can help to increase the effectiveness of the team.[24]

In Belbin's study the best runner-up teams were those containing cooperative, stable extroverts. The team members were mostly Team Workers and Resource Investigators with Coordinators as a secondary team role. The team members did not contain a great spread of team types. Additionally, the team had a good level of mental ability and they did not seem to suffer from lack of having a Monitor Evaluator or Plant.[25]

It is not necessarily the case that each team needs every role to function well. It depends on the team and the task. It is not always good to have a Completer Finisher at the beginning of a project. It is necessary to get the right balance between the person's preference and their qualifications.[26]

It appears that the bigger the group, the greater the unseen pressures that make for conformity.[27] After finding out which roles are needed in the team, the ideal size of the team has to be calculated. A group consisting of ten or eleven members is a frequently used and effective size of team. This number is deemed to be large enough to give adequate variety in the possible range of social permutations but small enough to allow the syndicate to retain a sense of intimate group identity.[28]

However, for decision-making, meetings around the table, thrashing out ideas and policies and giving everyone the opportunity to chip in with comments, a group of ten or eleven is not always optimal. In this case, a six-man team is very stable and an intimate circle. Additionally, a team of six can also have a wide range of skills and team roles and the company could achieve a high degree of balance.[29]

There is a risk of inefficient work when large or medium-sized teams are involved in high rates of activity. In such cases a team of four has some level of intimacy,

---

[24] Cf. Belbin (2004), p. 79 ff.
[25] Cf. Belbin (2004), p. 96.
[26] Cf. Costello (2011), p. 26; Recklies (2001), w.p.
[27] Cf. Belbin (2004), p. 105.
[28] Cf. Belbin (2004), p. 107.
[29] Cf. Belbin (2004), p. 107 ff.

involvement and excitement which six-man groups would never achieved.[30] At least, the ideal team-size depends on the task, but in many published studies it consists of about three to six members.[31]

The most successful teams, the so-called winning teams, are those which are a mixture of different types of people, people with a range of different talents and characteristics.[32] However, it can quiet difficult to put such a mixed team together. The selector needs to have highly developed skills, because any disturbances within the team can easily upset the balance. It might be better to form groups out of team-oriented, stable extroverts, well disciplined, and with good mental abilities. These teams perform well and produce consistently good results. A further advantage is that these team members can be combined and recombined with other teams without losing much efficiency.[33]

3 Phases of Team Development

In 1965, Bruce W. Tuckman created the various phases of team development, see Figure 2. He observed small groups at work or in learning environments and he described different the stages which groups go through. He argued that every group has to experience every stage of the team development to achieve maximum effectiveness.[34] Later, in 1977, Tuckman and Mary Ann Conover Jensen extended this model. The phases described the stages of team development of forming, storming, "norming", performing and adjourning, see Figure 3.[35] Tuckman's model has become 'the most predominantly referred to and most widely recognized in organizational literature.'[36] This model reflects the way people were working together, helping each other to

---

[30] Cf. Belbin (2004), p. 109 f.
[31] Cf. Water/Ahaus/Rozier (2008), p. 511; Groen (2006), p. 45.
[32] Cf. Belbin (2004), p. 97; belbin.com (2012 d), w.p.
[33] Cf. Belbin (2004), p. 103.
[34] Cf. Staggers/Garcia/Nagelhout (2008), p. 477.
[35] Cf. Tuckman (1965), p. 384-399; Tuckman/Jensen (1977), p. 419-427; Bonebright (2010), p. 111; Edison (2008), p. 14.
[36] Miller (2003), p. 122.

understand what was happening in the development process, and to support consultants in a way which can be used to predict the stages of growth in groups.[37]

Tuckman hypothesized a model with four stages. Each stage needed to be successfully navigated in order to reach effective group functioning.[38] In the following chapters the stages will be described in detail.

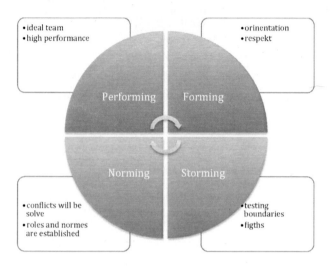

• ideal team
• high performance

• orinentation
• respekt

Performing   Forming

Norming   Storming

• conflicts will be solve
• roles and normes are established

• testing boundaries
• figths

Figure 2: Tuckman's Stages of Team Development[39]

3.1 The Stages of Team Development

The first stage of the model is characterized by insecurity. The team members test their behavior and they want to make a good impression. The group has to become oriented and create group roles. The group is dependent on the leader, who structures, initiates and decides the actions taken by the team.[40]

Storming:

---

[37] Cf. Bonebright (2010), p. 111; Rickards/Moger (2000), p. 277.
[38] Cf. Bonebright (2010), p. 113.
[39] Own illustration, based on: Tuckmann (1965).
[40] Cf. Bonebright (2010), p. 113; Rickards/Moger (2000), p. 277; Staggers/Garcia/Nagelhout (2008), p. 478.; Chaneski (2009), w.p.

After the group has established itself, friction within the team can come to the fore. This phase represents a time of intergroup conflict. The team members compete with each other. There is a lack of unity and the members polarize around interpersonal issues. They move into unknown areas of interpersonal relations and they want to retain their security.[41] The "group members become hostile toward one another and toward a therapist or trainer as a means of expressing their individuality and resisting the formations of group structure."[42] The team resists against the task in an emotional way.[43]

Norming:

In the third phase the team establishes roles and norms. The group members accept the idiosyncrasies of the other members and express personal opinions. In this stage the group becomes an entity. The members seek to perpetuate the group. The conflicts of the task are avoided. The group cooperates together.[44]

Performing:

The fourth stage is the final stage of the original model. The team structure is adept and played roles will enhance the task activities. In this phase the team is a problem-solving instrument. The team is flexible and functional. The team concentrates on the task, solving the problem and is oriented to achieving its goals. The energy is channeled into the task.[45]

---

[41] Cf. Bonebright (2010), p. 114; Rickards/Moger (2000), p. 277; Staggers/Garcia/Nagelhout (2008), p. 478 ff.; Chaneski (2009), w.p.
[42] Tuckman (1965), p. 386.
[43] Cf. Bonebright (2010), p. 114.
[44] Cf. Bonebright (2010), p. 114; Levasseur (2011), p. 205; Rickards/Moger (2000), p. 277; Staggers/Garcia/Nagelhout (2008), p. 481 ff.; Chaneski (2009), w.p.
[45] Cf. Bonebright (2010), p. 114; Rickards/Moger (2000), p. 277; Staggers/Garcia/Nagelhout (2008), p. 484 f.; Chaneski (2009), w.p.

Figure 3: The Revised Model of Team Development[46]

Adjourning:

In 1977 Tuckman and Mary Ann Conover Jensen extending this model of team development, identified a fifth stage, "adjourning", see Figure 3. This This phase, the separation of the group, "is an important issue throughout the life of the group."[47] In this phase the team have achieve their goals and they need to recognize their achievements and move on separately.[48]

3.2   Limitations of the Model

In Tuckman's original model from 1965 there are some limitations. The first is that there is no representative sample of settings where small groups' development processes are likely to occur. The therapy-group settings were also significant overrepresented. But the model also works well beyond its original framework;[49] Cassidy produced a study between 1990 and 2001 to explore how the stages work outside of therapy-groups. She found out, that they all fit into a five-stage framework.[50]

Rickards and Moger identified a further limitation. They noticed out that Tuckman did not describe how groups change over time. They identified two significant references to task performance. The first one relates to how the model fails to address the effects of team development on creativity in problem solving. The second is that the model does not discuss some of the failures in achieving success in task performance and the ability to show outstanding performance. Rickards and Moger asked two important questions;

---

[46] Source: Rickards/Moger (2000), p. 277.
[47] Bonebright (2010), p. 114.
[48] Cf. Staggers/Garcia/Nagelhout (2008), p. 485.
[49] Cf. Bonebright (2010), p. 115.
[50] Cf. Cassidy (2007), p. 416.

what if the storm stage never ends?, and what is needed to exceed performance norms?[51]

Gersick also asked the question, as to whether such models adequately address mechanisms for change over a group's lifespan, or when and how a group moves from one stage to the next. She also noted that staged-based models, such as the team development of Tuckman, are limited because they frame groups as closed systems but do not address outside influences on group development.[52]

4 Conclusion

As the second chapter showed which team roles exist and what team roles are, it described how a winning team be built up. The most important fact is that the usefulness of a team depends on the task to be executed. Belbin found out that not only does the group with the sharpest analytical minds and the most experience perform better than other teams, it can also occur that they often perform worse. The most successful teams, the so-called winning teams, are those which are a good mix of different people with a wide range of different characteristics and talents.[53]

In the third chapter the phases of team development were discussed. Each stage of development has to pass by before the group can enter in to the next stage. The team performs best in the stage of performing. This is the fourth stage. In the previous three stages the team members become oriented, testing their boundaries and solving the conflicts in the team.[54]

Teamwork is becoming more and more important for companies and it is therefore important that businesses focus on assembling the best possible teams. Furthermore, companies should train or hire project managers, so that they can select and lead the teams with their expertise and knowledge.[55]

---

[51] Cf. Rickards/Moger (2000), p. 281 ff.
[52] Cf. Gersick (1998), p. 11.
[53] Cf. Belbin (2004), p. 103; Staggers/Garcia/Nagelhout (2008), p. 477.
[54] Cf. Bonebright (2010), p. 113 f.
[55] Cf. Sueddeutsche.de (2012), w.p.

Bibliography

Aritzeta, A./Ayestaran, S./Swailes, S. (2005): Team Role Preference and Conflict Management Styles, in: The International Journal of Conflict Management, Vol. 16, No. 2, pp. 157-182.

belbin.com (2012 a): BELBIN FAQ, available from: http://www.belbin.com/content/page/5895/BELBIN(uk)-2011-FAQs.pdf, [accessed: June 25th, 2012].

belbin.com (2012 b): BELBIN TEAM ROLES, available from: http://www.belbin.com/rte.asp?id=8, [accessed: August 28th, 2012].

belbin.com (2012 c): BELBIN Team Role Summary Descriptions, available from: http://www.belbin.com/content/page/49/BELBIN(uk)-2011-TeamRoleSummaryDescriptions.pdf, [accessed on: August 29th, 2012].

belbin.com (2012 d): BELBIN History & Research, available from: http://www.belbin.com/rte.asp?id=3, [accessed on: September 11th, 2012].

Belbin, M. (1999): Improving the Job, in: Training Journal, November, p. 32.

Belbin, M. (2000): Beyond the Team, Oxford.

Belbin, M. (2004): Management Teams: Why They Succeed or Fail, 2nd Edt., Oxford.

Belbin, M. (2008): Der Belbin-Ratgeber für Erfolg im Arbeitsleben, Wörrstadt.

Belbin, M. (2010): Team Roles at Work, 2nd Edt., Oxford.

Blenkinsop, N./Maddison, A. (2007): Team Roles and Team Performance in Defence Acquisition, in: Journal of Management Development, Vol. 26, No. 7, pp. 667-682.

Bonebright, D. (2010): 40 Years of Storming: A Historical Review of Tuckman's Model of Small Group Development, in: Human Resource Development International, Vol. 13, No. 1, pp. 111-120.

Cassidy, K. (2007): Tuckman revisited: Proposing a New Model of Group Development for Practitioners, in: Journal of Experimental Education, Vol. 29, No. 3, pp. 413-417.

Chaneski, W. (2009): The Stages Teams Go Through, in: Modern Machine Shop, Vol. 82, No. 8, pp. 34-36.

Costello, M. (2011): Team Weaver – Meredith Belbin's Explanation of How Teams Work Has Stood the Test of Time and Spread Across the Globe, in: People Management, January 2011, pp. 26-27.

Edison, T. (2008): The Team Development Life Cycle – A New Look, in: Defence & AT-L, pp. 14-17.

Eickenberg, S. (2006): Mitarbeitertypologie und Teambildung, Lohmar.

Groen, R. (2006): The Crisis Team Exercise, in: Training Journal, December 2006, pp. 45-48.

Levasseur, R. (2011): People Skills: Optimizing Team Development and Performance, in: Interfaces, Vol. 41, No. 2, pp. 204-208.

Manangementpraxis.de (2012): Bedeutung von Teamarbeit in der heutigen Zeit, available   from: http://www.managementpraxis.ch/praxistipp_view.cfm?nr=3637&stichwort=Teamarbei t, [accessed on: September 18th, 2012].

Miller, D. (2003): The Stages of Group Development: A Retrospective Study of Dynamic Team Processes, in: Canadian Journal of Administrative Sciences, Vol. 20, No. 2, pp. 121-134.

Recklies, D. (2001): Die richtige Zusammensetzung des Teams – Belbin's Team Roles, available   from: http://www.themanagement.de/HumanResources/Teamrollen.htm, [accessed on: September 14th, 2012].

Rickards, T./Moger, S. (2000): Creative Leadership Process in Project Team Development: An Alternative to Tuckman's Stage Model, in: Journal of Management, Vol. 11, No. 4, pp. 273-283.

Senior, B. (1997): Team Roles and Team Performance: Is there 'really' a link?, in: Journal of Occupational and Organizational Psychology, Vol. 70, pp. 241-258.

Staggers, J./Garcia, S./Nagelhout, E. (2008): Teamwork Through Team Building: Face-to-Face to Online, in: Business Communication Quarterly, Vol. 71, No. 4, pp. 472-487.

Sueddeutsche.de (2012): Unternehmen im Wandel: Projektteams sind die neuen Abteilungen, available from: http://www.sueddeutsche.de/karriere/unternehmen-im-wandel-projektteams-sind-die-neuen-abteilungen-1.1225415, [accessed on: September 18th, 2012].

Tuckman, B. (1965): Development Sequence in Small Groups, in: Psychological Bulletin, Vol. 63, No. 6, pp. 384-399.

Tuckman, B./Jensen, M. (1977): Stages of Small Group Development Revisited, in: Group and Organizational Studies, Vol. 2, pp. 419-427.

Water, H. v. d./Ahaus, K./Rozier, R. (2008): Team roles, team balance and performance, in: Journal of Management Development, Vol. 27, No. 5, pp. 499-512.

ITM-Checklist

Complex of Topics	The Sine Qua Non of Success	Comments/Suggestions
General Economics	Which macroeconomic relevance is inherent in the topic?	The macroeconomic relevance is, that soft skills improve the cooperation between employees in a company and between companies when they work together in teams. So companies work more efficiency on the market and more successful.

If employees work in cross-company's projects, e.g. working groups between supplier and distributor or customer, then the collaboration between them improved and so they have more economic success.

The more successful the companies are, the better get the economy as whole. |
| Strategic Management | How is the topic's strategic relevance to be evaluated, especially concerning the aspects of securing existence, competitive advantages, tying up resources, sustainability, and risk? | The strategic relevance as related to the aspects of securing existence, is because of soft skills, the working climate is getting better. And if the company has a good working climate, they could easier keep the employees in the company or get new good employees because of the good reputation.

The strategic relevance concerning to competitive advantages are, that because of good teams they can effect good processes and with the processes the can achieve |

		good work results. When the companies have good teams, they can easier solve problems, especially through unofficial channels, with save a lot of time and money.
Marketing	What advantages and disadvantages arise out of the suggestions for marketing measures, external impact, and the company's general productivity? Which measures should be taken concerning internal and/or external marketing?	The advantages of good teams, good soft skills and of good working climate in companies are, that even the employees, who are not in sales office, talk good about the company when they talk with other persons about the company. So this is a good reputation for the company. Also because of good teamwork and good processes, the company has good working results, so the reputation of the company is good, too. A disadvantage may be, if employees like to talk about the company, they also could talk too much about the company and so disclose interne data's about the company. The measures a company should do, is to build up and promote soft skills and good teamwork.
Financial Management	What criteria have to be considered when choosing appropriate terms of financing? Which risks are there	The risk for working in groups is, that bad teams may stick together and talk about problems instead of solving them. So the company has high costs and no or not satisfied solutions.

	and what kind of coverage do you suggest?	Additionally if companies train their employees in soft skills, the trainings are expensive and eventually the company has no direct visible success.
Human Resource Management	Which personnel consequences (quantitative or qualitative) result from the suggestions?	The personnel consequences in qualitative way are, that the companies should train or hire skilled personnel, who is able to assemble groups and lead them through a project. So the working results get better, because of efficient teamwork. In quantitative way the companies should eventually hire some project managers to develop and lead the teams. A high level of soft skills leads to efficient work, eventually in smaller teams, and so fewer resources needed.
Business Law	Which legal fields are affected by the suggestions? What has to be arranged in order to create legal security from the company's point of view?	The legal fields are mainly in data protection law, especially in cooperation of teams in between different companies. In this case the companies should made mutual confidentiality and non-disclosure agreement.
Research Methods/ Decision	What sources of information should be practiced in order to stay up to date in the field of	The sources are current professional literature, seminaries, trainings and coaching's.

Making	topics? Which decision criteria should be practiced on the choice of alternatives?	The decision criteria are the current requirements or abuses in the company.
Soft Skills/ Leadership	Which demands does the realization of the suggestions require of the responsible managers? What leadership behavior is expedient?	The responsible manager has to choose the right people for the team, this is a very hard task, because the manager has to estimate the team members and how they fit in their role. But before the manager found out, which people he chooses, he has to find out, which roles are required for the team. For teams the right leadership behavior does not exist. Because every team has other demands and tasks. So the leadership has to adjust his leadership style to the situation, which is needed. But he also should consider, that his leadership style is a role model for his employees.

Teamwork is the most important factor in achieving success in competition for companies. Teamwork should support companies to operate effectively and flexibly in the market. For employee's teamwork is also important; in every job advertisement teamwork is required. And the higher an employee rises on the career ladder, the more important teamwork becomes. (...)

www.grin.com

Document Nr. V266388
http://www.grin.com
ISBN 978-3-656-56457-7

9 783656 564577